EVOLVE

WORKBOOK

Samuela Eckstut

1 B

CAMBRIDGE
UNIVERSITY PRESS

CAMBRIDGE
UNIVERSITY PRESS & ASSESSMENT

Shaftesbury Road, Cambridge CB2 8EA, United Kingdom

One Liberty Plaza, 20th Floor, New York, NY 10006, USA

477 Williamstown Road, Port Melbourne, VIC 3207, Australia

314–321, 3rd Floor, Plot 3, Splendor Forum, Jasola District Centre, New Delhi – 110025, India

103 Penang Road, #05-06/07, Visioncrest Commercial, Singapore 238467

Cambridge University Press & Assessment is a department of the University of Cambridge.

We share the University's mission to contribute to society through the pursuit of education, learning and research at the highest international levels of excellence.

www.cambridge.org
Information on this title: www.cambridge.org/9781108411912

© Cambridge University Press & Assessment 2019

This publication is in copyright. Subject to statutory exception and to the provisions of relevant collective licensing agreements, no reproduction of any part may take place without the written permission of Cambridge University Press & Assessment.

First published 2019

20 19 18 17 16 15 14 13 12 11 10 9

Printed in Mexico by Litográfica Ingramex, S.A. de C.V.

A catalogue record for this publication is available from the British Library

ISBN 978-1-108-40521-8 Student's Book
ISBN 978-1-108-40503-4 Student's Book A
ISBN 978-1-108-40914-8 Student's Book B
ISBN 978-1-108-40522-5 Student's Book with Practice Extra
ISBN 978-1-108-40504-1 Student's Book with Practice Extra A
ISBN 978-1-108-40915-5 Student's Book with Practice Extra B
ISBN 978-1-108-40894-3 Workbook with Audio
ISBN 978-1-108-40859-2 Workbook with Audio A
ISBN 978-1-108-41191-2 Workbook with Audio B
ISBN 978-1-108-40512-6 Teacher's Edition with Test Generator
ISBN 978-1-108-41062-5 Presentation Plus
ISBN 978-1-108-41201-8 Class Audio CDs
ISBN 978-1-108-40791-5 Video Resource Book with DVD
ISBN 978-1-108-41200-1 Full Contact with DVD
ISBN 978-1-108-41152-3 Full Contact with DVD A
ISBN 978-1-108-41410-4 Full Contact with DVD B

Additional resources for this publication at www.cambridge.org/evolve

Cambridge University Press & Assessment has no responsibility for the persistence or accuracy of URLs for external or third-party internet websites referred to in this publication, and does not guarantee that any content on such websites is, or will remain, accurate or appropriate. Information regarding prices, travel timetables, and other factual information given in this work is correct at the time of first printing but Cambridge University Press & Assessment does not guarantee the accuracy of such information thereafter.

CONTENTS

7 NOW IS GOOD 50

8 YOU'RE GOOD! 58

9 PLACES TO GO 66

10 GET READY 74

11 COLORFUL MEMORIES 82

12 STOP, EAT, GO 90

Extra activities 98

1   VOCABULARY: Activities around the house

A   **Cross out the words that do _not_ complete the sentences.**

1 I clean _____ on the weekend.	the bathroom	the kitchen	~~my hair~~
2 We cook _____ every day.	coffee	dinner	breakfast
3 He washes _____ at night.	the computer	his hair	the dog
4 She brushes _____ in the morning.	her hair	her bed	her teeth
5 I take _____ every morning.	a bath	my room	a shower
6 They do _____ in the evening.	their breakfast	the dishes	their homework
7 You help _____ a lot.	your friends	your home	your mother

2   GRAMMAR: Present continuous statements

A   **Write the _–ing_ form of the verbs.**

1 chat   _chatting_
2 do   _____
3 eat   _____
4 get   _____
5 go   _____
6 have   _____
7 play   _____
8 run   _____
9 shop   _____
10 study   _____
11 take   _____
12 work   _____

B **Complete the sentences with the present continuous form of the verbs in parentheses ( ).**

1 I'm chatting _____ (chat) on the phone right now.

2 We _____ (do) the dishes in the kitchen.

3 Sara and Tomas are at a store. They _____ (shop) for new furniture.

4 Riu is in the bathroom. He _____ (take) a shower.

5 The girls are in the park. They _____ (run).

6 This game isn't boring. We _____ (have) fun.

7 The children are in bed, but they _____ (get) up now.

8 I'm in the kitchen. I _____ (eat) lunch.

3 GRAMMAR AND VOCABULARY

A **Complete the sentences with the affirmative (+) or negative (–) form of the present continuous.**

1 I usually take a shower at 7:30 a.m. It's 9:00 now.
I'm not taking _____ a shower right now.

2 Sandra doesn't cook lunch on weekdays. It's noon on Tuesday. Sandra _____ lunch at the moment.

3 Benjamin and Deb do the dishes after dinner. It's after dinner. They _____ the dishes.

4 Harry always brushes his teeth after he eats. It's after lunch. He _____ his teeth now.

5 Eva always helps her parents on the weekend. It's Saturday. She _____ her parents right now.

6 My family and I never clean our house on a weekday. It's Monday. We _____ our house.

B **Circle the correct words.**

1 I sometimes *take* / *am taking* a bath at night.

2 Ruiz *doesn't cook* / *isn't cooking* dinner right now.

3 The students often *do* / *are doing* their homework before class.

4 I always *am brushing* / *brush* my teeth in the morning and at night.

5 My family and I never *do* / *are doing* the dishes together.

6 Katya *cleans* / *is cleaning* her room right now.

C **Look at the sentences in exercise 3B. Then write what you are doing (or not doing) right now.**

1 _____ I'm not taking a bath right now. _____

2 _____

3 _____

4 _____

5 _____

6 _____

TEXTING ON THE RUN

1 VOCABULARY: Transportation

A **Match the questions (1–6) with the answers (a–f).**

1 Are you driving to work? ___c___
2 Are you walking to work? _____
3 Are you at the movie theater? _____
4 What are you studying? _____
5 Are you coming home now? _____
6 Where are you riding your bike? _____

a Yes. I'm waiting for Tom.
b No. My office isn't near my house.
c Yes, I am. I drive every day.
d I'm riding it to the park.
e Yes, but I'm shopping in the mall first.
f I'm not studying right now. I'm reading.

2 GRAMMAR: Present continuous questions

A **Read the words and write questions.**

1 you / do / homework / right now?   *Are you doing your homework right now?*
2 your friends / play / soccer / right now?   _____
3 your friend / send / you / a text message?   _____
4 you and your friends / learn / English?   _____
5 you / listen / to music / right now?   _____

B **Answer the questions so they are true for you.**

1 _____Yes, I am._____
2 _____
3 _____
4 _____
5 _____

C **Read the short conversations. Write the questions for B.**

1 **A** Lisa isn't waiting for her husband.

   B *Who is she waiting for?*

   A She's waiting for her brother.

2 **A** I'm not going to work right now.

   B _____

   A I'm going to the supermarket.

3 **A** Yoko's in the kitchen.

   B _____

   A She's studying for her exam. And drinking coffee!

4 **A** The boys are carrying some big bags.

   B _____

   A Because they're helping their aunt.

5 **A** I'm helping my daughter with her homework.

   B _____

   A Because she has an exam on Friday.

6 **A** My children are in the park.

   B _____

   A No, not soccer. They're playing basketball.

3 GRAMMAR AND VOCABULARY

A **You are on a train. People are talking on their cell phones. Write present continuous questions for the answers. Use the words in the box.**

go	on the bus	ride your bike	~~take the train~~	wait for your friend	walk

1 **A** *Are you taking the train?*   **B** Yes, I am. I'm visiting my friend.

2 **A** _____   **B** No, I'm not. She's here.

3 **A** _____   **B** No, I'm not. I'm on the train.

4 **A** _____   **B** I'm walking to the movie theater.

5 **A** _____   **B** I'm going to a party.

6 **A** _____   **B** No. My brother has my bike.

B **You are on a bus. People are talking on their cell phones. Write two conversations. Use the words in the box in exercise 3A.**

1 **A** _____

   B _____

2 **A** _____

   B _____

A NEW LIFE

1 FUNCTIONAL LANGUAGE: Asking how things are going

A **Put the phone conversation in the correct order.**

_____	**Jesse**	Really? Me, too.
1	**Jesse**	Hello.
_____	**Jesse**	Hey, Gustavo!
_____	**Jesse**	Not bad, thanks. How are you?
_____	**Gustavo**	How are you doing?
_____	**Gustavo**	Hi, Jesse. It's Gustavo.
_____	**Gustavo**	I'm fine. I'm doing my homework right now.

2 REAL-WORLD STRATEGY: Reacting to news

A **Read the sentences. Check (✓) good news, bad news, or ordinary news. Write** _Oh, Oh wow!,_ **or** _Oh no._

	Good news	Bad news	Ordinary news	Reaction
1 I love my new job!				
2 I'm helping my son with his homework.				
3 My grandmother is 100 years old.				
4 There are no rooms at the hotel today.				
5 I have one brother and one sister.				
6 I'm 20 minutes late for class.				

3 FUNCTIONAL LANGUAGE AND REAL-WORLD STRATEGY

A **Complete the conversation.**

Anna ¹____ Hello.

Paul Hi, Anna. ²_____ Paul.

Anna ³_____, Paul. How ⁴_____ you?

Paul Good. How are you ⁵_____?

Anna ⁶_____ fine, thanks. Are you at home?

Paul No. I'm driving to work.

Anna On Sunday?

Paul Yeah. I'm working on Sundays these days.

Anna Oh, ⁷_____! Why?

Paul I have a new job on weekends.

Anna ⁸_____. Do you like it?

Paul Yeah, I love it!

Anna Oh, ⁹_____! That's great.

B **Read about Sylvia and Rafael. How many children does Sylvia have? What is Rafael's bad news?**

Sylvia and Rafael are cousins. They live in Florida. Sylvia's children are six, nine, and fourteen years old. Sylvia is always busy – at work and at home. Rafael has some bad news. His wife, Pearl, is not in Florida right now. She is working in California.

C **Sylvia and Rafael are talking. Write their conversation. Use the information in exercise 3B.**

_____   _____

_____   _____

_____   _____

_____   _____

_____   _____

7.4 CHAOS!

1 READING

A **SCAN** **Read the blog. When does the restaurant close?**

The Life of a Chef: A to Z by Chef Andy
B is for Busy!

[Thursday, January 15, 5:30 a.m.] I'm having breakfast at the restaurant. This is my favorite time of the day. There are no people here.

[Thursday, January 15, 6:00 a.m.] Now there are ten people in the restaurant. They're drinking coffee and chatting. The same ten people come every day from 6:00 to 7:00. Then they take the 7:10 train to work.

[Thursday, January 15, 8:30 a.m.] Here are the moms and dads with small children. They're walking to the restaurant. Now they're opening the door. Oh, no! The children are running in the restaurant. I don't like that.

[Thursday, January 15, 9:15 a.m.] I'm cooking today's lunch. The restaurant's servers, Nick and Alicia are helping me in the kitchen.

[Thursday, January 15, 11:15 a.m.] I'm eating lunch with Nick and Alicia. We always eat before people come for lunch.

[Thursday, January 15, 12:00 p.m.] It's noon now. People are waiting at the door. There are 20 people!

[Thursday, January 15, 2:30 p.m.] There usually aren't a lot of people in the restaurant in the afternoon. We're cleaning the kitchen and the tables in the dining area.

[Thursday, January 15, 4:30 p.m.] I'm cooking dinner. Mac and Pilar are helping me now. We are cooking food for 50 people! The restaurant closes at 11 p.m. It's a very busy day. But people love my food, so I love my job!

B **READ FOR DETAILS** **Read the blog again. Then complete the chart with the times.**

5:30 a.m.	Andy is having breakfast.		Andy is cooking lunch.
	Ten people are drinking coffee and talking.		Andy and two people are having lunch.
	Parents are coming to the restaurant with their children.		People are coming for lunch at the restaurant.
			Andy is cooking dinner.

2 LISTENING

A 🔊 **7.01** **LISTEN FOR SUPPORTING DETAILS** **Listen to Andy talk about his job. Choose the correct answers.**

1 How many people does Andy cook for every day?

   a 100   **b** four   **c** 200

2 How many days a week is the restaurant open?

   a seven   **b** three   **c** four

3 Why do the people like the restaurant?

   a because they're not cooking at home   **b** because the restaurant is busy

   c because they're not at work

4 What does Andy do in his free time?

   a cooks at home   **b** eats in restaurants   **c** helps his friends

3 WRITING

A **Match 1–6 with a–f. Then write sentences below. Add *too* or *also* and use the correct punctuation.**

1 I like Nick and Alicia. _____f_____ a I cook dinner. (too)
2 My job is busy. _____ b They're playing with things. (also)
3 The children are running in the restaurant. _____ c I'm a writer. (too)
4 I cook breakfast and lunch. _____ d They come for dinner. (also)
5 Mr and Mrs Garcia come for breakfast on Friday. _____ e I work a lot of hours. (also)
6 I'm a chef. _____ f I like Mac and Pilar. (too)

1 I like Nick and Alicia. I like Mac and Pilar, too. _____
2 _____
3 _____
4 _____
5 _____
6 _____

B **Add *And, But*, or *Also* to the sentences below. Use the correct punctuation.**

1 I like the blog. ___And OR Also,___ I think the comments are interesting.
2 The writer has a busy life. _____ he has fun.
3 She works in a Mexican restaurant. _____ she goes to school at night.
4 Clara and Hugo really like the Couch Café. _____ they think it's expensive.

C **Write a blog post about a day in your life. Give your blog a title (for example, *F is for Fun*). Write about what you do at different times of the day. What is your favorite time of the day? Why?**

CHECK AND REVIEW

Read the statements. Can you do these things?

UNIT 7	Mark the boxes. ☑ I can do it. ❓ I am not sure.		If you are not sure, go back to these pages in the Student's Book.
		I can …	
VOCABULARY	☐	use words about activities around the house.	page 66
	☐	use transportation words.	page 68
GRAMMAR	☐	use the present continuous in statements.	page 67
	☐	ask questions in the present continuous.	page 69
FUNCTIONAL LANGUAGE	☐	start a phone call.	page 70
	☐	react to news.	page 71
SKILLS	☐	write a blog about things happening now.	page 73
	☐	use *and, but*, and *also*.	page 73

8.1   SHE LIKES MUSIC, BUT SHE CAN'T DANCE!

1   VOCABULARY: Verbs to describe skills

A   **Look at the pictures and complete the sentences. Use the correct form of the verbs in the box.**

dance	draw	fix things	paint	play the guitar	read music
sing	skateboard	surf	snowboard	speak two languages	~~swim~~

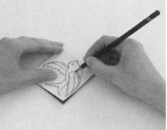

1 Matt _____swims_____ every week.

2 Jorge is an artist and _____ beautiful pictures.

3 Sidney _____ for people.

4 Natalia is Mexican-American. She _____.

5 Renato goes to the beach every weekend and _____.

6 Ben is in a music class and _____ well.

7 Jaime _____ in the mountains in winter.

8 Aiko often goes to the park and _____.

9 Lorena _____ in a band.

10 Paola _____ with her cousin at family parties.

11 Sergei _____ his favorite music in the morning.

12 Emma _____ with her friends after school.

2 GRAMMAR: *can* and *can't* for ability; *well*

A Read the text. Circle *can* or *can't* to complete the sentences.

My family is from the United States. My brother and I ¹*can* / *can't* speak English and Spanish. My brother lives in France now, and he ²*can* / *can't* speak French, too. My mom only speaks English – she ³*can* / *can't* speak other languages. My dad ⁴*can* / *can't* speak other languages, but he ⁵*can* / *can't* read music. He loves his piano!

We have other skills, too. My mom ⁶*can* / *can't* fix things, for example the car, or our bikes. They always work well. My brother ⁷*can* / *can't* draw well, and he ⁸*can* / *can't* paint well, too. I love his pictures! I ⁹*can* / *can't* sing well – my brother says I'm not very good. But I ¹⁰*can* / *can't* dance – I love it!

B Write sentences with *can*. Use the verbs in the box and *well*.

cook	draw	drive	play music	~~play soccer~~	speak English

1 Soccer players *can play soccer well.*
2 Bus drivers _____ .
3 A chef _____ .
4 English teachers _____ .
5 An artist _____ .
6 People in a band _____ .

3 GRAMMAR AND VOCABULARY

A Complete the chart for you. Then write questions and answers with *can* or *can't* and the words in parentheses ( ).

	dance	draw	fix things	paint	play the guitar	read music	ride a bike	sing	skateboard	snowboard	speak two languages	surf	swim
Carla	✔	✗	✔	✗	✔	✔	✔	✔	✗	✗	✔	✗	✔
Tony	✔	✔	✔	✔	✗	✗	✔	✗	✔	✗	✔	✔	✔
You													

1 (Carla / play the guitar)   *Can Carla play the guitar? Yes, she can.*
2 (Tony / sing)   _____
3 (Carla and Tony / snowboard)   _____
4 (Carla and Tony / speak two languages)   _____
5 (Carla / surf)   _____
6 (Tony / paint)   _____
7 (you / read music)   _____
8 (you / fix things)   _____

B Look at the answers. Write questions about people you know. Use the verbs in exercise 3A.

1 *Can your mother swim?* Yes, she can.   4 _____ No, she can't.
2 _____ Yes, he can.   5 _____ No, they can't.
3 _____ No, he can't.   6 _____ Yes, they can.

HAPPY WORKERS = GREAT WORKERS?

1 VOCABULARY: Work

A **Complete the sentences with the words in the box.**

company	coworkers	have a meeting	office
take a break	think	work hard	workers

I work for a big ¹ _____company_____ . Its name is Verulia. There are 250 ² _____ in my company. Some people work in the capital city, but 50 of us work in Gardon, near my home. I like my ³ _____ . They are very friendly. The ⁴ _____ is nice because it is near a park. I usually ⁵ _____ at 10:30 for half an hour. I go for a walk in the park. Sometimes 10 or 15 of us ⁶ _____ in the park. It's really good because we ⁷ _____ of great ideas outside. I ⁸ _____ – sometimes for six days a week – but I love my job!

2 GRAMMAR: *can* and *can't* for possibility

A **Complete the sentences with *can* or *can't*.**

1 It's possible to swim in the lake.

We *can swim in the lake.* _____

2 It's not possible to surf there.

You _____

3 It's not possible to use my cell phone in the mountains.

I _____

4 It's possible to ride our bikes in the park.

We _____

5 Maria doesn't walk a lot. It's possible to take the bus.

She _____

6 It's not possible for a dog to go in a restaurant.

A dog _____

B Write questions about your English class.
Use *can* or *can't* and the words in parentheses ( ).
Then write answers for the questions.

1 (be late for class)

Can you be late for class?

No, I (OR we) can't.

2 (speak your language in class)

_____

_____

3 (ask your teacher questions)

_____

_____

4 (use your cell phone in class)

_____

_____

5 (when / have a meeting with your teacher)

_____

_____

6 (what / do on your break)

_____

_____

3 GRAMMAR AND VOCABULARY

A Look at the chart. How are New Tech Company and Best Tech Company different? Write sentences about each company. Use *can* and *can't*.

	New Tech Company	Best Tech Company
work at home or in the office	✔	
work in the office every day		✔
30 hours a week + 10 minute coffee break every day		✔
50 hours a week + breaks when you want	✔	
meetings in the office three times a week		✔
Skype meetings every month	✔	

1 At New Tech Company, you can work from home or in the office.

2 _____

3 _____

4 _____

B Do you want to work at New Tech Company or Best Tech Company? Write your answer.
Give two or three reasons.

_____

_____

_____

8.3 ARE YOU THE RIGHT PERSON?

1 FUNCTIONAL LANGUAGE: Giving and asking for opinions

A **Put the words into the correct order to make questions.**

1 Do / have happy workers?/ that / you / think / great companies

Do you think that great companies have happy workers?

2 Why / friends are important? / you / do / think

_____

3 you / technology / a good thing? / is / think / Do

_____

4 fun? / you / think / Do / school / is

_____

5 a job? / Why / you / think / want / do / people

_____

B **Match the questions from exercise 1A with the answers below.**

a _____ Yes. I think technology is changing the world. It's good.

b _____ I think people want a job because they want money.

c _____ Yes, I do. I think that good companies always have happy workers.

d _____ No. I think school is boring.

e _____ I think friends are important because they are fun and interesting.

C **Answer the questions so they are true for you. Give your opinion. Use _I think so_ or _I don't think so_.**

1 Are you good at sports? _____ *I don't think so.*

2 Are you a good worker? _____

3 Are you good at video games? _____

4 Are you a good coworker? _____

5 Are you good at teamwork? _____

2 REAL-WORLD STRATEGY: Explaining and saying more about an idea

A **Circle _a_ or _b_ to complete the sentences.**

1 I think this is a great company. I mean,
   - **ⓐ** It's a good place to work.
   - **b** I'm a really good worker.

2 We love our dog. I mean,
   - **a** her name is Kiki.
   - **b** she's always fun and happy.

3 My coworkers are great. I mean,
   - **a** we work well together.
   - **b** we work in the same office.

4 I'm not very good at soccer. I mean,
   - **a** I watch soccer on TV, but I can't *play* soccer.
   - **b** I watch soccer with my friends a lot.

3 FUNCTIONAL LANGUAGE AND REAL-WORLD STRATEGY

A **Bill has an interview for a job at a restaurant. Use the expressions in the box to complete the conversation.**

> Do you think that …   I don't think so.   I mean, …   I think so.

Chef Are you the right person for this job?

Bill Yeah. [1]_____

Chef Why are you a good server?

Bill Because on weekends, I go to different restaurants with my friends, and I see a lot of servers. The good servers are friendly. I'm friendly, too.

Chef OK. [2]_____ it's important to work well with other servers?

Bill [3]_____ . I mean, servers don't work with other servers.

Chef Really? In my restaurant, teamwork is important. The servers work with the chefs in the kitchen.

Bill Oh.

Chef Our busy days are Friday, Saturday, and Sunday. Can you work then?

Bill I can't work on Saturday and Sunday. [4]_____ I'm busy on weekends. But I can work on Tuesday, Wednesday, and Thursday.

B **Is Bill is the right person for the job? Why or why not?**

_____

_____

C **Write a conversation between the chef and a woman, Sofia. The chef thinks Sofia is the right person for the job.**

_____

_____

_____

_____

_____

_____

_____

_____

_____

_____

_____

_____

8.4 | COMPUTERS AND OUR JOBS

1 | LISTENING

A   🔊 **8.01** **LISTEN FOR DETAILS** Listen to part of a podcast about robots. What do Emily and Joel think? (Circle) the correct answer.

Emily and Joel *think / do not think* that a robot can be a child's friend.

B   🔊 **8.01** **LISTEN FOR SUPPORTING DETAILS** Listen again. What is good about robots for children? Check (✓) the things Emily and Joel say.

1 Children can play games with robots.   ☐
2 Children can learn about technology from robots.   ☐
3 Children can play soccer with robots.   ☐
4 Robots and children can have birthday parties.   ☐
5 Robots are not real friends.   ☐
6 Children can do things with robots all day.   ☐

2 | READING

A   Read the article. Then choose the correct title. (Circle) 1, 2, or 3.

1 New Robots
2 Our Grandparents' Problems
3 Robots for Our Grandparents

Companies now have talking robots for grandparents. Sometimes, our grandparents do not live with other people. They do not talk to other people every day and they don't see their friends often. This is a problem, and the new robots can help.

Elena Cho is an example. She is an old woman. She doesn't live with her family. But now, she has a talking robot. It can tell her about new books or interesting movies. Also, it can play music for Elena. Her robot knows her favorite songs and singers.

Elena Cho says, "My robot is not a friend, but I like it very much."

B   Read the article again. Check (✓) the correct sentences.

1 Some grandparents do not live with other people.   ✔
2 New robots can help grandparents.   ___
3 Elena Cho's robot goes to the movies with her.   ___
4 Elena Cho's robot plays her favorite music.   ___
5 Elena doesn't like her robot.   ___

A Read three people's online comments about the podcast. Find the quotes from Emily and Joel. Change the punctuation for the quotes.

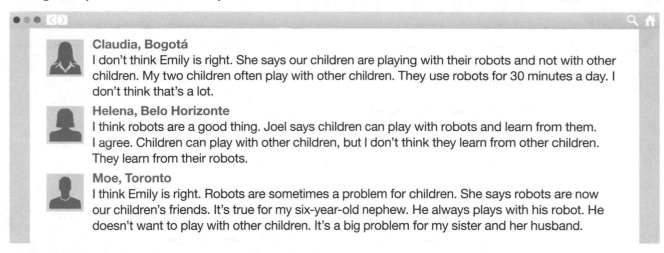

Claudia, Bogotá
I don't think Emily is right. She says our children are playing with their robots and not with other children. My two children often play with other children. They use robots for 30 minutes a day. I don't think that's a lot.

Helena, Belo Horizonte
I think robots are a good thing. Joel says children can play with robots and learn from them. I agree. Children can play with other children, but I don't think they learn from other children. They learn from their robots.

Moe, Toronto
I think Emily is right. Robots are sometimes a problem for children. She says robots are now our children's friends. It's true for my six-year-old nephew. He always plays with his robot. He doesn't want to play with other children. It's a big problem for my sister and her husband.

B Look at the sentences about robots for old people. Change the sentences to quotes. Use *says* or *said* and the correct punctuation.

Informal writing:

1 Elena Cho: I like my new talking robot.

_____

2 Elena Cho's son: The robot helps my mother a lot.

_____

Formal writing:

3 Ronaldo Benson: Our company makes robots for grandparents.

_____

4 Doctor Wu: Robots are good for grandparents because their families don't see them every day.

_____

C Write an online comment. Give your opinion about robots for grandparents.

CHECK AND REVIEW

Read the statements. Can you do these things?

UNIT 8	Mark the boxes. ☑ I can do it. ? I am not sure. I can …	If you are not sure, go back to these pages in the Student's Book.
VOCABULARY	☐ use verbs to describe skills.	page 76
	☐ use words about work.	page 78
GRAMMAR	☐ use *can* or *can't* for ability.	page 77
	☐ use *well*.	page 77
	☐ use *can* or *can't* for possibility.	page 79
FUNCTIONAL LANGUAGE	☐ ask for and give opinions.	page 80
	☐ explain and say more about an idea.	page 81
SKILLS	☐ write an online comment.	page 83
	☐ use quotations for other people's words.	page 83

1　VOCABULARY: Travel

A　**Complete the sentences with the words in the box.**

boat	country	plane	ranch
tickets	tour	town	~~vacation~~

1　Silvia and Raúl aren't working. They are on _____vacation_____ .

2　Raúl loves animals. He's on a farm in the _____, away from the city.

3　Silvia loves the ocean. She goes on a _____ on the water.

4　Silvia and Raúl buy _____ for the museum. They are $25 each.

5　Silvia doesn't like animals. A _____ is not a good place for her.

6　Silvia lives in a small _____. It has 10,000 people.

7　Silvia and Raúl go on a _____ of the museum. A woman tells them about the interesting art.

8　Silvia sits next to Raúl on the _____. She looks out the window and sees buildings and trees.

2　GRAMMAR: *This* and *These*

A　**Complete the conversations. Use *this* or *these* and the words in the box.**

museum	photos	seats
your hotel	your tickets	~~your train~~

1　**A** Is _____this your train_____ ?

　B Yes, it is. We're going home.

2　**A** Are _____ ?

　B Yes. We need them for the movie.

3　**A** _____ cool.

　B Yes. They are from our vacation.

4　**A** Is _____ ?

　B Yes, our room is very nice!

5　**A** Wow, _____ comfortable.

　B Yes, they are.

6　**A** _____ interesting.

　B Yes. It has a lot of beautiful pictures.

GRAMMAR AND VOCABULARY

A   Look at the pictures from people's vacations. Imagine you are writing messages about each trip. Write two or three sentences for each picture. Use *this* or *these*. How many words from the box can you use?

boat   country   farm   ranch   plane   ticket   tour   town   vacation

1   We're on a bike tour. There are many interesting places on the tour. It's not boring!

2

3

SAN FRANCISCO, HERE WE COME

1 VOCABULARY: Travel arrangements

A **Cross out the words that do <u>not</u> complete the sentences.**

1 We have to arrive _____ at 2 p.m.	at our destination	at the airport	~~on a trip~~
2 They are buying _____.	friends	some coffee	tickets
3 The flight _____ at 10 a.m.	arrives	leaves	stays
4 We are _____ my aunt's house.	checking in at	staying at	traveling to
5 Our _____ is from June 15 to July 1.	destination	trip	vacation
6 We can check in at the _____.	airport	hotel	museum
7 We _____ on the plane for 12 hours.	arrive	fly	travel
8 People can buy plane tickets _____.	at the airport	online	on a flight

2 GRAMMAR: *like to, want to, need to, have to*

A **Circle the correct answers.**

1 My husband has a business trip this week. He *has to* / *likes to* go to Boston.

2 This is our favorite restaurant. We *like to* / *need to* go there for lunch on Sunday.

3 My brother is studying to be a doctor. He *wants to* / *needs to* study for five years.

4 This camera is not in the stores. You *want to* / *have to* buy it online.

5 Can we take the bus to the mall? I don't *have to* / *want to* drive.

6 My friends and I are learning Chinese. *We want to* / *need to* go to China on vacation next year.

7 I *like to* / *have to* eat cookies for breakfast, but I know it's bad for me.

8 My friend *wants to* / *likes to* work at a big technology company. She has an interview there next week!

B Complete the sentences with affirmative (+) or negative (–) forms of *have to*, *like to*, *need to*, or *want to*. Sometimes there are two correct answers.

1 It's 10 a.m. My flight is at 12 p.m. I'm late! I ___*need to* OR *have to*___ go to the airport.

2 My sister _____ go on vacation with our parents. She likes to travel with her friends.

3 Jason's very hungry. He _____ eat dinner now.

4 Sari _____ travel on the subway. It's busy and hot.

5 My parents' car is very old. They _____ buy a new car.

6 We're planning our next vacation. We _____ go to a lot of interesting places.

3 GRAMMAR AND VOCABULARY

A **Write sentences that are true for you.**

1 have / check in / three hours before my flight

   I have to check in three hours before my flight at the airport near my city.

2 like / fly

   _____

3 have / buy plane tickets online

   _____

4 like / stay at hotels

   _____

5 need / arrive / at the bus stop 15 minutes early

   _____

6 want / work / at an airport

   _____

7 need / leave / home before 8:00 a.m.

   _____

8 like / take / trips to places near my home

   _____

9 want / travel / to New York

   _____

1 FUNCTIONAL LANGUAGE: Asking for missing information and clarification

A **Correct <u>four</u> mistakes in the conversations.**

1 A Excuse me. Where~~/~~ ^is^ the women's restroom?

   B It's over there, near the door.

2 A Excuse me. What time the bus to San Diego leave?

   B It leaves at 11:15 a.m.

3 A Excuse me. How much this guide book?

   B It's $12.99.

4 A Excuse me. I need buy a ticket to Bogotá. How much is it?

   B A bus ticket $147.

B **Put the conversation in the correct order.**

____	A	And for a child? Is it the same price?
1	A	Excuse me. How much is one ticket?
____	A	Then one ticket for me and one ticket for my son, please.
____	A	Where are seats 10A and 10B?
____	B	Tickets are $15.
8	B	They're on the right.
____	B	OK. Your seats are 10A and 10B.
____	B	No, it isn't. Tickets for children are $5.

2 REAL-WORLD STRATEGY: Asking someone to repeat something

A **Check (✓) <u>two</u> correct ways to ask someone to repeat something.**

1 Sorry, repeat, please. ____

2 Sorry, can you repeat that, please? ____

3 Sorry, what you say? ____

4 Sorry, can you say that again? ____

3 FUNCTIONAL LANGUAGE AND REAL-WORLD STRATEGY

A **Mia is at a store. She talks to a clerk. Use the information below to write their conversation.**

1 Mia wants to know the price of the flowers.
2 The clerk says a price.
3 Mia wants to know the price of a plant, too.
4 The clerk says a price for the flowers and the plant together.
5 Mia doesn't understand.
6 The clerk repeats the information.

7 Mia understands. Now she wants to know where a good café is.
8 The clerk gives directions.
9 Mia doesn't understand.
10 The clerk repeats the directions.
11 Mia thanks the clerk.
12 The clerk finishes the conversation.

1 **Mia** *Excuse me. How much are the flowers?*
2 **Clerk** _____
3 **Mia** _____
4 **Clerk** _____
5 **Mia** _____
6 **Clerk** _____
7 **Mia** _____
8 **Clerk** _____
9 **Mia** _____
10 **Clerk** _____
11 **Mia** _____
12 **Clerk** _____

71

1 READING

A **SKIM** Skim the article. Check (✓) the things the article mentions.

☐ horses   ☐ museums   ☐ hotels

☐ countries in South America   ☐ food

GLOSSARY
ride a horse (v) sit on a horse

South American ranch vacations ✈

Do you like animals and nature? Do you want to travel and meet people? Why not visit a *gaucho* ranch?

A *gaucho* ranch is a very big farm with horses and other animals. The workers there are called *gauchos*. They are really good with horses. People can visit *gaucho* ranches and learn about the farm and the animals.

Can you ride a horse well? The *gauchos* can take you on a tour of the ranch.

Do you want to learn to ride a horse? The *gauchos* can help you!

There are *gaucho* ranches in South America, for example in Argentina, Bolivia, Chile, and Uruguay. You can visit for a week, or you can work on a *gaucho* ranch for a month. Some ranches even have one-day tours.

You don't have to ride a horse every day. You can also walk around the ranch and see all the interesting plants and animals.

Maybe you don't want to go to the country, but you're interested in ranches. Some towns near ranches have *gaucho* museums. One *gaucho* museum is only 90 minutes from Buenos Aires. You can go there and learn a lot about *gaucho* life. Also, the museum is free!

So, go to a *gaucho* ranch and have a great vacation!

An Argentinian *gaucho* on his horse

B Read the article again. Answer the questions. Write complete sentences.

1 Where does a gaucho work? _____

2 What countries have gaucho ranches? _____

3 How long can you stay at a gaucho ranch? _____

4 What can you learn about in a gaucho museum? _____

2 LISTENING

A 🔊 **9.01** **LISTEN FOR DETAILS** Listen to Ella talk about her vacation. Does she like it?

B 🔊 **9.01** **LISTEN FOR SUPPORTING DETAILS** Listen again. Choose the correct answer.

1 Ella is visiting _____.

   a a ranch   **b** an island   **c** a museum

2 What does Ella think about the people there?

   a They are interesting.   **b** They are different.   **c** They are friendly.

3 What can Ella do in the afternoon?

   a cook lunch   **b** go for a walk   **c** talk to her mother

4 Next year, Ella wants to _____.

   a come with her mother   **b** stay longer   **c** get a bigger room

3 WRITING

A   **Read the advice below. Complete the paragraphs with affirmative (+) and negative (–) imperative verbs in the box.**

drive   eat   go x2   ~~read~~   ride   take

How to plan your ranch vacation

Ranch vacations in Argentina are great, but ¹_____read_____ the online reviews before you go. ²_____ from October to December or from April to June. These are good times to visit. ³_____ from January to March. It can be very hot. Some ranches are hundreds of miles from Buenos Aires. ⁴_____ to the ranches in a car. It's very far. ⁵_____ a plane and then a taxi.

Is this your first time on a horse? You can have lessons on the ranch. They're not expensive. Or can you ride a horse well? ⁶_____ to a different part of the ranch every day. Ranches are really big. You need to visit for a week or two!

⁷_____ a lot at lunch. Dinner is a big meal, and the food is great!

B   **Change the formal sentences to informal sentences. Use imperatives.**

1   You need to come for a week.   *Come for a week.*

2   You can visit the place in August.   _____

3   You have to take a taxi.   _____

4   You need to eat a big breakfast   _____

C   **Think about a place you like. Write about what people can do and see there. Use imperatives to give advice.**

CHECK AND REVIEW

Read the statements. Can you do these things?

UNIT 9	Mark the boxes. ☑ I can do it. ❓ I am not sure. I can …	If you are not sure, go back to these pages in the Student's Book.
VOCABULARY	☐ use travel words. ☐ use words for travel arrangements.	page 86 page 88
GRAMMAR	☐ use *this* and *these*. ☐ use *like to, want to, have to,* and *need to.*	page 87 page 89
FUNCTIONAL LANGUAGE	☐ ask for and give missing information. ☐ ask someone to repeat something.	page 90 page 91
SKILLS	☐ write a description of a place. ☐ use imperatives to give advice.	page 93 page 93

1 VOCABULARY: Going out

A **Use the words in the box to complete the conversation.**

eat	get	go	have	look at	meet	take x2

A What do you usually do on the weekend? I need ideas!

B I visit the mall and ¹_____ shopping. Sometimes I ²_____ together with friends. What about you?

A I like to go to the museum near my home and ³_____ art. I like to ⁴_____ a walk outside, too. I often go to the park.

B The park is great! You can ⁵_____ a picnic in the park. It's fun to ⁶_____ outside!

A Good idea! I never have picnics in the park. Usually I ⁷_____ my husband out to dinner at our favorite restaurant. But not this weekend.

B Oh? Why not? Where is he?

A He's in New York right now. He's going to be home next week. I want to ⁸_____ him at the airport.

2 GRAMMAR: Statements with *be going to*

A **Imagine that it is 10 a.m. on Thursday, July 6. Look at the future plans below. Replace the underlined words with future time expressions from the box. You won't use all the words.**

next month	on Saturday	this weekend	next Saturday	this afternoon
this year	next week	this month	tomorrow	next weekend
this Saturday	tonight	next year	this week	

1 I'm going to swim <u>in six hours</u>.
   I'm going to swim this afternoon.

2 The doctor is going to call <u>in 24 hours</u>.

3 Miriam is going to have a party <u>on August 6</u>.

4 We're going to meet our friend <u>in two days</u>.

5 We're going to buy the tickets <u>in 10 hours</u>.

6 They aren't going to have a picnic <u>in seven days</u>.

B **Write sentences with *be going to*.**

1 It's Monday today. I meet my friends every Tuesday.
   I'm going to meet my friends tomorrow _____.

2 Felipe takes a walk every night.
   _____ tonight.

3 Marco and his friends go to the mall every weekend.
   _____ next weekend.

4 Sara doesn't want to take a trip next year.
   _____ next year.

5 Kate and her coworkers take a break every day at 11:00.
   _____ this morning at 11:00.

6 I have class every Tuesday.
   _____ on Tuesday.

3 GRAMMAR AND VOCABULARY

A **Look at Simon's plans for Friday, Saturday, and Sunday. Write sentences about what he is going to do.**

Thursday	Friday	Saturday	Sunday
Today!	Meet my friend at the airport	Picnic at the beach	Go shopping at the mall
	Take my friend out for dinner		Free time

1 *On Friday, Simon is going to meet his friend at the airport.* _____

2 _____

3 _____

4 _____

5 _____

B **Write five true sentences about you. Use the words in exercise 1A, *be going to*, and future time expressions from exercise 2A.**

1 *I'm going to meet my sister tomorrow afternoon. Then we're going to go shopping.*

2 _____

3 _____

4 _____

5 _____

6 _____

BUT IT'S SUMMER THERE!

1 VOCABULARY: Clothes; seasons

A **Cross out the word that does <u>not</u> belong in each sentence.**

1 jeans	pants	~~T-shirt~~	**4** shorts	sweater	skirt
2 shorts	coat	hat	**5** sweater	shirt	boots
3 dress	shoes	boots	**6** pants	skirt	jeans

B **Read the descriptions of clothes. Which season is each person talking about? Write words in the box.**

dry season	fall	rainy season	spring	summer	winter

1 There's no rain, and it's hot! I wear shorts every day. _____dry season_____

2 It's very cold! I'm wearing a coat and a hat. _____

3 I'm on the beach. I'm wearing shorts and a T-shirt, and no shoes! _____

4 It's not summer, but I can see new flowers. I'm wearing a shirt and pants.
   I don't need to wear a sweater. _____

5 There's a lot of rain, but it's not cold. I'm wearing a coat and my big boots. _____

6 I'm wearing a dress. I have a coat, but I'm not wearing it. The next season is winter. _____

2 GRAMMAR: Questions with *be going to*

A **Read the sentences and complete the questions. Then answer the questions so they are true for you. Write short answers.**

1 I'm not going to get together with friends this weekend.
   Are you going to get together _____ with friends next weekend?
   _____Yes, I am. OR No, I'm not._____

2 My friend isn't going to meet me tonight.
   _____ you tomorrow?
   _____

3 My family and I aren't going to be on vacation this month.
   _____ next month?
   _____

4 My friends aren't going to take me out to dinner this week.
   _____ you out to dinner next week?
   _____

5 My teacher isn't going to work this summer.
   _____ next summer?
   _____

6 I'm not going to buy a car in the spring.
   _____ next fall?
   _____

B **Write questions for the answers. Use *What*, *When*, *Where*, or *Who*.**

1 A Who are you going to meet?

   B I'm going to meet my cousins.

2 A _____

   B The class is going to take a break in 20 minutes.

3 A _____

   B The stores are going to open at 9 a.m.

4 A _____

   B We're going to go shopping at the mall.

5 A _____

   B My brother is going to buy a TV.

6 A _____

   B I'm going to visit my parents.

3 GRAMMAR AND VOCABULARY

A **Use the words to write questions. Then write true answers. Use *be going to*.**

1 who / you / visit / this fall

   Who are you going to visit this fall?

   I'm going to visit my friend in Canada.

2 who / go / with / you / on your trip

   _____

   _____

3 what clothes / you / take / on your next trip

   _____

   _____

4 when / you / buy / boots

   _____

   _____

5 what / country / you / travel / in the rainy season?

   _____

   _____

6 where / your friend / wear / her new dress

   _____

   _____

7 where / your cousin / buy / new pants

   _____

   _____

8 when / you / wear / a sweater

   _____

   _____

LET'S MEET AT THE HOTEL

1 FUNCTIONAL LANGUAGE: Making and responding to suggestions

A **Look at the conversations. Circle the correct responses.**

1 A There's a good Chinese restaurant near here.
   B a Why don't we eat Chinese food?
      b Why don't we walk there?

2 A I don't want to cook dinner tonight.
   B a Let's eat at home.
      b Let's go to a restaurant.

3 A It's a beautiful day outside.
   B a Why don't we take a walk?
      b Why don't we watch a movie?

4 A The museum is 15 kilometers from here.
   B a Let's walk to the museum.
      b Let's take a bus.

5 A Let's eat outside.
   B a Yes, we do.
      b Good idea.

6 A Why don't we have a picnic on Sunday?
   B a Sorry, I'm busy.
      b No, we don't.

7 A Why don't we meet at the hotel?
   B a Yes, sure.
      b Let's meet at the hotel.

8 A Let's go to the beach.
   B a I'm sorry.
      b OK, sounds good.

2 REAL-WORLD STRATEGY: Saying why you can't do something

A **Look at Amy's week below. Then write her responses to sentences 1–5. Use *have to*.**

Things to do next week:

Monday — Friday — work from 8 a.m.–4 p.m.

Monday — doctor, 6 p.m.

Tuesday — make dinner for my family

Saturday — Aunt Beatriz's party

Sunday — study

1 Let's go to the mall Monday evening.   **Amy** *I'm sorry, but I can't. I have to go to the doctor.*
2 Why don't we meet for lunch on Friday?   **Amy** _____
3 Let's have dinner together on Tuesday.   **Amy** _____
4 Why don't we get together on Saturday?   **Amy** _____
5 Let's go to the beach on Sunday.   **Amy** _____

FUNCTIONAL LANGUAGE AND REAL-WORLD STRATEGY

A **Alex and Jay are making plans for their friend Keiko's birthday. Put the sentences in the correct order.**

_____	**Keiko**	Hello.
_____	**Alex**	Good idea. Let's go to the new Korean restaurant on First Street. It's really good.
_1_	**Alex**	So, it's Keiko's birthday on Friday.
_____	**Keiko**	I'm sorry, but I can't. I'm busy then. My family is going to have a birthday party for me. Hey, why don't you and Alex come to the party?
_____	**Alex**	Hi, Keiko. It's Alex. Jay and I are talking about your birthday. We want to take you out for dinner. Why don't we meet at the new Korean restaurant next Friday?
_____	**Jay**	OK, great. Let's call Keiko and ask her.
_____	**Jay**	Oh, yeah! Why don't we take her out to dinner for her birthday?
_9_	**Alex**	Thanks, Keiko. We love birthday parties. We can take you out to dinner next weekend.
_____	**Alex**	Sure. I have her number on my phone. I'm calling her now …

B **Read the information below. Then write a conversation.**

You are making plans with two friends for next weekend. Talk about what you are going to do and when you are going to do it. You and your friends are not free at the same time. Find a time to get together.

_____

_____

_____

_____

_____

_____

_____

_____

10.4 A 24-HOUR CITY

1 LISTENING

A 🔊 **10.01** **LISTEN FOR DETAILS** Listen to Susana talk about her trip to Stockholm, Sweden. Check (✓) the things Susana says about Stockholm.

☐ It's famous.   ☐ There are a lot of things to do.

☐ There are old buildings.   ☐ It's not hot.

B 🔊 **10.01** **LISTEN FOR SUPPORTING DETAILS** Listen again. Put the things to do in the order Susana says them. Cross out the sentences that she does not talk about.

_____ **a** go to a museum   _____ **e** go shopping and eat something

_____ **b** go to the beach   _____ **f** go for a bike ride

_____ **c** go to an island   __1__ **g** tour famous places

_____ **d** find a place to go dancing   _____ **h** have a picnic

2 READING

A **Read the article about Midsummer Day in Sweden. Write *T* if the sentence is true or *F* if the sentence is false.**

Midsummer Day is a very important day in Sweden. There is sun in the day *and* night. The holiday is on June 24, but the activities are always on the weekend. People wear holiday clothes for the day's activities, and they wear flowers, too. Children and adults dance and play games. They eat different foods – and the first strawberries of summer. Midsummer is also a time of love. Girls and young women take home seven different flowers. When they go to sleep on Midsummer Night, they see who their husband is going to be. Midsummer Day is really an important day.

strawberries

Midsummer Day in Sweden

__T__ **1** It is always in June.   _____ **3** People wear different clothes.

_____ **2** Midsummer Day is only for children.   _____ **4** Flowers are important.

3 WRITING

A Read the online invitation. <u>Underline</u> <u>six</u> full forms. Change the full forms to contractions.

Event Beach party!
Host Brianna
When? Saturday, June 20
Where? Miami Beach

Message from Brianna

Jeff's
<u>Jeff is</u> going to be 25 on June 10. We are going to have a beach party for him. Be at Miami Beach near Fifth Street at 6:00 p.m. We are going to have a big picnic. Then we are going to go out. It is going to be a fun night! Do not tell Jeff about the party. He does not know about it.

B Circle the contractions in the sentences. Write *F* if the sentence is formal. Write *I* if the sentence is informal.

1 There's going to be dancing.   I

2 Jenny is going to send the invitation.   _____

3 I am going to ask 30 people to come to the party. _____

4 We're going to have a lot of fun.   _____

5 Do not be late.   _____

C Imagine it's a friend's birthday party. Write an invitation for their party. Describe what you are going to do. Use contractions.

CHECK AND REVIEW

Read the statements. Can you do these things?

UNIT 10	Mark the boxes. ☑ I can do it. ? I am not sure. I can …	If you are not sure, go back to these pages in the Student's Book.
VOCABULARY	☐ use words for going out activities. ☐ use words for clothes and seasons.	page 98 page 100
GRAMMAR	☐ use *be going to* in statements. ☐ use *be going to* in *yes/no* and information questions.	page 99 page 101
FUNCTIONAL LANGUAGE	☐ make and respond to suggestions. ☐ say why I can't do something.	page 102 page 103
SKILLS	☐ write an online invitation. ☐ use contractions.	page 105 page 105

1 VOCABULARY: Describing people, places, and things

A **Match the adjectives (1–5) with their opposites (a–e).**

1 awful   *e*   a boring
2 exciting _____   b noisy
3 fast   _____   c old
4 new   _____   d slow
5 quiet   _____   e wonderful

B **Cross out the word that people do <u>not</u> use with *beautiful* and *cute*.**

1 **beautiful**   day   girl   man   picture   woman
2 **cute**   class   dog   dress   little boy   little girl

2 GRAMMAR: Statements with *was* and *were*

A **Complete the sentences with *was*, *wasn't*, *were*, or *weren't*.**

1 I'm tall now, but I _____*wasn't*_____ a tall child.

2 My grandparents are always home now, but in 2015, they _____ at work.

3 We're in the same class now, but we _____ in the same class last year.

4 Gabriel is in college now, but in 2016, he _____ in high school.

5 I'm not on vacation now, but I _____ on vacation last week.

6 School is fun now, but it _____ fun before.

7 Yessica is good at basketball now, but she _____ good last year.

8 You're here now, but you _____ here at 10 o'clock.

9 My friends are in college now, but they _____ last year.

10 Sergio _____ at our company last year, but now he is.

11 It _____ nice and quiet in my house this morning because my children _____ asleep.

12 I _____ in the office all week, but I'm not today because it's Sunday!

B **Read the postcard. Then complete the sentences with *was*, *wasn't*, *were*, or *weren't*.**

July 10

Hi Leonor,

Tony and I are having a wonderful vacation. We're at the beach right now. He's swimming, and I'm writing this postcard! This beach is beautiful, but it's noisy. There are a lot of really cute children here, and they're playing near us. But that's OK. It's a beautiful day, and we're having a great time.

How are you?

Love,

Ines

1 It's August now. Ines _____ on vacation in July.

2 Ines's parents _____ with her.

3 Ines and Tony _____ at the beach on July 10.

4 The beach _____ quiet.

5 There _____ a lot of children.

3 GRAMMAR AND VOCABULARY

A **Read the sentences. Then write two sentences that are the opposite. Use *wasn't* or *weren't* for A. Use *was* or *were* for B.**

1 I was quiet in class.

   A I wasn't quiet in class.   B I was noisy in class.

2 I was awful at sports in school.

   A _____   B _____

3 My school was in an old neighborhood.

   A _____   B _____

4 New books were boring for me.

   A _____   B _____

5 My first job was wonderful.

   A _____   B _____

6 My friends and I were noisy.

   A _____   B _____

7 My first computer was new.

   A _____   B _____

8 I was a good student.

   A _____   B _____

11.2 OUR OLD PHONE WAS GREEN

1 VOCABULARY: Colors

A **Unscramble the color words.**

1 ckbal _____
2 earong _____
3 twihe _____
4 dre _____
5 llowye _____
6 gary _____
7 lbeu _____
8 pkni _____
9 neerg _____
10 nrowb _____
11 lepurp _____

B **Complete the sentences so they are true for you. Use color words from exercise 1A.**

1 My cell phone is _____.
2 My favorite shirt is _____.
3 My bag is _____.
4 I'm wearing _____ clothes today.
5 I don't like the color _____.

2 GRAMMAR: Questions with *was* and *were*

A **Complete the *yes/no* questions with *was* or *were*. Then answer the questions so they are true for you. Use short answers.**

1 I wasn't at home on Sunday.

   Were you at home on Saturday? _____   Yes, I was. OR No, I wasn't.

2 My family and I weren't on vacation in August.

   _____ on vacation in June? _____

3 I wasn't in class on Tuesday.

   _____ in class on Wednesday? _____

4 My cousins weren't in college in 2016.

   _____ in college in 2017? _____

5 My friends weren't busy on Saturday.

   _____ busy on Friday? _____

6 My teacher wasn't at work on Sunday.

   _____ at work on Monday? _____

B **Use the words to write questions with *was* or *were*. Then answer the questions so they are true for you.**

1 what / your first teacher's name

   <u>What was your first teacher's name?</u>   <u>My first teacher's name was Ms. Song.</u>

2 where / your first school

3 how old / you / in 2005

4 what color / your first cell phone

5 where / you / on Saturday night

6 who / with you / on the weekend

3 GRAMMAR AND VOCABULARY

A **Read the questions about when you were a child. Correct the mistake in each question. Then answer the questions so they are true for you.**

1 What things <s>was</s> ^{were} brown in your home?

   <u>Our kitchen table and chairs were brown.</u>

2 What your favorite color was?

3 What color were your favorite toy?

4 Was your shoes always black?

5 Your desk was white?

6 Are there gray walls in your first home?

11.3 | I HAVE NO IDEA

1 FUNCTIONAL LANGUAGE: Expressing uncertainty

A **Erica and Chris are at a party. Erica asks questions about the people she sees. Circle the correct words to complete the conversation.**

Erica Who's that man over there?

Chris ¹I'm *not / no* sure. ²I *think / know* he's Alma's brother.

Erica OK. And who's the woman next to him?

Chris Oh, that's Jamie's wife. Her name is Mischa, ³I *know / think*.

Erica Right. Where's Alma? It's her birthday party and I can't see her!

Chris ⁴I have *no / not* idea!

Erica There's Jamie. ⁵*Maybe / Yeah* Jamie can tell us!

2 REAL-WORLD STRATEGY: Taking time to think

A **Chris needs time to think about Erica's questions. Write *Let me think*, *Uh*, or *Um* in the conversation. There can sometimes be more than one answer.**

Erica Do you need more food, Chris?

Chris _____, I'm not hungry, thanks.

Erica What time do you want to leave?

Chris _____. Maybe in an hour?

Erica Do you want to dance?

Chris _____, yeah!

3 FUNCTIONAL LANGUAGE AND REAL-WORLD STRATEGY

A **Read sentences 1–5. Write a conversation between you and a friend. Use the words in the box in your friend's answers.**

I have no idea.	Uh, …	I don't know.	I think …
Maybe …	Um, …	Let me think.	I'm not sure.

1 You want to know Leonardo DiCaprio's age in *Titanic*.

      You   How old was Leonardo DiCaprio in *Titanic*?

      Your friend   Uh, I don't know.

2 You want to know where Leonardo DiCaprio's parents are from.

      You _____

      Your friend _____

3 You want to know the name of the actor in a TV show.

      You _____

      Your friend _____

4 You want to know when a movie was popular.

      You _____

      Your friend _____

5 You want to know who is in a famous band.

      You _____

      Your friend _____

1 READING

A   **SKIM** **Read the article. Find <u>three</u> reasons why people keep things.**

Why do we keep things?

Old toys. Old music. Old soccer balls. Why are they so important? Why do we keep them? Here are three reasons:

Our feelings

5   Maybe your favorite toy when you were a child was from your grandparents. You don't play with the toy now. You never see it. But you still want to keep it. Why? Because it's from your grandparents. You love them very much. So you
10   keep the toy.

Money

Do you have your parents' old music? Maybe the music was five dollars in the 1970s. Maybe it is going to be 50 or 100 dollars in 20 years. Sometimes we keep things because we can get money for them in the future.

15   ### The future

Why are you keeping your old soccer ball or your old guitar? You don't need them now. You don't play soccer or the guitar. But maybe your son or daughter is going to be a great soccer player or a wonderful guitar player. You're keeping them for your children.

B   **READ FOR DETAIL** **Read words 1–5 below. Circle the words in the article. Then match the words with their meanings (a–g). You don't need to use all the meanings.**

1 it (*line 7*)	_g_	**a** children	**f** things
2 them (*line 9*)	___	**b** grandparents	**g** toy
3 it (*line 13*)	___	**c** music	
4 them (*line 14*)	___	**d** parents	
5 them (*line 18*)	___	**e** soccer ball or guitar	

2 LISTENING

A   ◀)) **11.01** **LISTEN FOR DETAILS** **Listen to the conversation. Write *T* for True and *F* for False.**

_____ **1** Tadeo and Jen are shopping for old things.

_____ **2** School wasn't very important for Tadeo.

_____ **3** Tadeo's teacher was good.

B   ◀)) **11.01** **LISTEN FOR SUPPORTING DETAILS** **Listen to the conversation again. What does Tadeo keep? Does he keep it because it's expensive, or because he loves it?**

3 WRITING

A **Read Ichiko's email. Write the correct topic sentences (a–c) for the paragraphs (1–3).**

> **a** There's a photo of you and me at the airport.
>
> **b** Do you remember our trip to Colombia in 2010?
>
> **c** I have a photo of you on the beach.

> Reply Forward ✉
>
> Hi Rafa,
>
> **1** _____
>
> We went to the beach in Santa Marta. We were there day and night because there were no hotels. It was great. It wasn't very expensive, and it was really beautiful. I'm writing to you because I have some pictures from the trip!
>
> **2** _____
>
> You're in the water 🌊 next to a really tall man, and you're wearing a new shirt. You were very cute. Do you remember the guy's name? I think he was from Canada. 🇨🇦
>
> **3** _____
>
> I'm wearing a long skirt with flowers. 🌼 The flowers on my skirt were red, yellow, and orange. Your shirt was pink and purple. I can't remember your shorts. They weren't very nice. Do you remember them? Do you have the photo? 📷
>
> Love,
> Ichiko

B **Read the sentences and check (✓) where emojis are correct.**

1 (At the doctor's office) Can the doctor see me tomorrow? 😲 _____

2 (On social media) I was at work until 10:30 last night. 😠 _____

3 (In a text message) Do you want to get together on the weekend? 😲 _____

4 (At school) Professor Marumi, I'm not going to be in class next week. 😠 _____

C **Write an email about a trip in the past. Use one paragraph for each idea. Write a topic sentence for each paragraph.**

CHECK AND REVIEW

Read the statements. Can you do these things?

UNIT 11	Mark the boxes. ☑ I can do it. ? I am not sure.	If you are not sure, go back to these pages in the Student's Book.
	I can …	
VOCABULARY	☐ use adjectives to describe people, places, and things.	page 108
	☐ use words for colors.	page 110
GRAMMAR	☐ use statements with *was* and *were*.	page 109
	☐ use questions with *was* and *were*	page 111
FUNCTIONAL LANGUAGE	☐ express uncertainty.	page 112
	☐ take time to think.	page 113
SKILLS	☐ use topic sentences in your writing.	page 115
	☐ write an email about an experience in the past.	page 115

12.1 BACKPACKING AND SNACKING

1 VOCABULARY: Snacks and small meals

A **Cross out the word that does <u>not</u> complete each sentence.**

1	I usually drink _____ juice with my breakfast.	apple	pineapple	~~potato~~
2	_____ comes from an animal.	Chicken	Beef	Soup
3	_____ is a dairy product.	Lamb	Cheese	Butter
4	_____ is made from grain.	a cracker	a pineapple	bread
5	_____ are fruit that grow on trees.	Potatoes	Coconuts	Oranges
6	I often have _____ for lunch.	soup	sandwiches	butter
7	I use _____ to make vegetable soup.	tomatoes	potatoes	apples

2 GRAMMAR: Simple past statements

A **Complete the sentences. Write the simple past form of the verbs.**

1 I like apples. I _____liked_____ apples when I was a child.

2 They don't go to the supermarket on Saturday. They _____ to the supermarket last Saturday.

3 Elena tries a different restaurant every month. She _____ a different restaurant last month.

4 We eat bread every day. We _____ bread yesterday.

5 I don't drink tea at night. I _____ tea last night.

6 Max always buys food on Sunday. He _____ food last Sunday.

B Change the affirmative (+) verbs so they're negative (–). Change the negative (–) verbs so they're affirmative (+).

1 I didn't eat beef. I _____ate_____ chicken.

2 I didn't drink coffee. I _____ tea.

3 Ramon liked the Chinese restaurant. He _____ the French restaurant.

4 The bus didn't arrive at 10:15. It _____ at 10:20.

5 We went to the supermarket. We _____ to the park.

6 We didn't stop for lunch. We _____ for a snack.

3 GRAMMAR AND VOCABULARY

A Write true affirmative (+) and negative (–) sentences about the past. Use the words in the box or your own ideas.

apple/apples	butter	cracker/crackers	potato/potatoes
banana/bananas	cheese	lamb	sandwich/sandwiches
beef	chicken	orange/oranges	soup
bread	coconut/coconuts	pineapple/pineapples	tomato/tomatoes

1 I / have / for dinner last night

I had chicken for dinner last night. I didn't have lamb.

2 I / buy / last week

_____

3 I / need / yesterday

_____

4 I / like / when I was a child

_____

5 I / want / last weekend

_____

6 I / eat / for breakfast this morning

_____

12.2 WHAT DID YOU EAT?

1 VOCABULARY: Food, drinks, and desserts

A **Find the words in the box in the word search.**

black beans	chocolate cake
cookies	eggs
fish	green beans
ice cream	juice
pizza	rice
soda	steak
water	

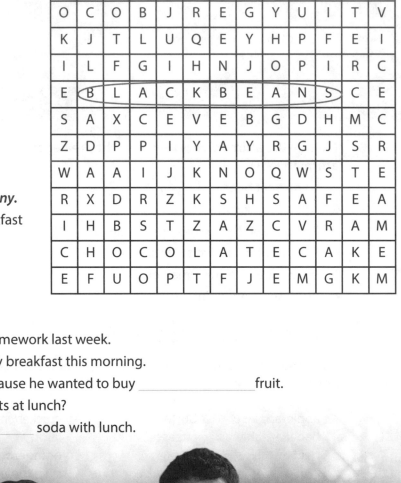

C	F	D	J	U	Z	G	R	Y	Z	K	W	P
O	F	J	A	G	P	R	H	S	O	D	A	L
O	C	O	B	J	R	E	G	Y	U	I	T	V
K	J	T	L	U	Q	E	Y	H	P	F	E	I
I	L	F	G	I	H	N	J	O	P	I	R	C
E	B	L	A	C	K	B	E	A	N	S	C	E
S	A	X	C	E	V	E	B	G	D	H	M	C
Z	D	P	P	I	Y	A	Y	R	G	J	S	R
W	A	A	I	J	K	N	O	Q	W	S	T	E
R	X	D	R	Z	K	S	H	S	A	F	E	A
I	H	B	S	T	Z	A	Z	C	V	R	A	M
C	H	O	C	O	L	A	T	E	C	A	K	E
E	F	U	O	P	T	F	J	E	M	G	K	M

2 GRAMMAR: Simple past questions; *any*

A **Complete the sentences with *some* or *any*.**

1 I didn't have _____*any*_____ breakfast this morning.

2 Armando wanted _____ cookies last night.

3 Did you eat _____ rice yesterday?

4 We didn't have _____ homework last week.

5 I had _____ juice with my breakfast this morning.

6 Manolo went to the supermarket because he wanted to buy _____ fruit.

7 Were there _____ desserts at lunch?

8 My children didn't drink _____ soda with lunch.

B Use the words to write questions about the past. Then answer the questions for you.

1 you / see / your friends / on the weekend

Did you see your friends on the weekend?   _No, I didn't. They were working._

2 you and your family / have / dinner at home / last Friday

_____   _____

3 what / you / eat / yesterday

_____   _____

4 how / they / hear / about the new café

_____   _____

5 he / drink / soda / at breakfast

_____   _____

6 you / go / to the movie theatre / after dinner

_____   _____

7 where / she / buy / the pineapples

_____   _____

8 you / take / your friends / to your favorite restaurant / last month

_____   _____

3 GRAMMAR AND VOCABULARY

A Write questions so the answers are true for you. Use the words in exercise 1A. You can use *any*.

1 **A** _Did you have any juice yesterday morning?_
  B Yes, I did. I had some orange juice.

2 **A** _____ last week?
  B No, I didn't. I don't like it, so I never drink it.

3 **A** _____ yesterday afternoon?
  B Yes, I did. I had some with lunch.

4 **A** _____ yesterday?
  B Yes, I did. I eat some every day.

5 **A** Where _____ ?
  B At the supermarket.

6 **A** How _____ ?
  B I didn't cook them. I never cook them.

12.3 PLEASE PASS THE BUTTER

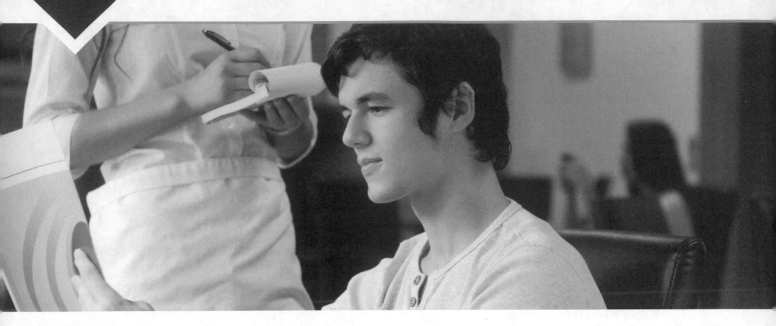

1 FUNCTIONAL LANGUAGE: Making and responding to offers and requests

A **Rewrite the sentences. Use *would like* or *'d like*.**

1 I want some fish, please.   *I would like (OR I'd like) some fish, please.*

2 Do you want some rice with the fish? _____

3 What do you want to drink? _____

4 When do you want the bread? _____

5 We want a table for six people. _____

6 Do you want a table near the window? _____

B **Circle the correct words.**

Server   Is everything OK?

Endo   ¹*I want water.* / *Can I have some water, please?*

Server   ²*Of course.* / *Thanks.* […] ³*Here you are.* / *This is your food.*

Endo   Thank you. I ⁴*like* / *'d like* some juice, too. ⁵*Do you have* / *How about* orange juice?

Server   I'm sorry. ⁶*We have* / *It's* orange soda but not orange juice. ⁷*Do* / *Would* you like some orange soda?

Endo   No, thanks. […] Luis, please ⁸*take* / *pass* the bread.

Luis   ⁹*Here you are.* / *No, thank you.*

Endo   Thanks.

2 REAL-WORLD STRATEGY: Using *so* and *really* to make words stronger

A **Add *so* or *really* to the sentences.**

1 This chocolate cake is good.

2 I want to go to the pizza restaurant.

3 My cell phone is cool.

4 Our apartment is small.

5 I need a vacation!

3 FUNCTIONAL LANGUAGE AND REAL-WORLD STRATEGY

A **Sandy is on a plane. Write the missing words in her conversation.**

Jake   Would you ¹_____like_____ something to drink?

Sandy   ²_____ you have juice?

Jake   We ³_____ apple juice and orange juice.

Sandy   ⁴_____ I have some apple juice, please?

Jake   ⁵_____ course. And what ⁶_____ you like for dinner? We ⁷_____ chicken or fish.

Sandy   I'd ⁸_____ the chicken, please.

Jake   Do you ⁹_____ green beans or black beans with the chicken?

Sandy   ¹⁰_____ like black beans, please.

Jake   ¹¹_____ you are.

Sandy   Thank you.

B **Imagine you are on a plane. You are going to eat and drink something. Write a conversation with the server. Say what you would like.**

_____

_____

_____

_____

_____

_____

_____

_____

_____

12.4   WHAT DID THE REVIEWERS SAY?

1   LISTENING

A 🔊 **12.01** **LISTEN FOR DETAILS** Listen to Mia and Seb talking about hotels. Which hotel do they choose – Astoria Hotel, Capital Hotel, or White Doors Hotel?

B 🔊 **12.01** **LISTEN FOR SUPPORTING DETAILS** Listen again. Match the hotels (1–3) with the correct information (a–f). You can use some information two times.

1 Astoria Hotel	_____	**a** It's expensive.
2 Capital Hotel	_____	**b** It's near the ocean.
3 White Doors Hotel	_____	**c** It's on a quiet street.

       d People need a car for this hotel.
       e The reviews of the hotel restaurant are good.
       f The hotel always has great reviews.

2   READING

A **Read the hotel review. Write (+) next to the things the reviewer liked. Write (–) next to the things the reviewer didn't like. Write (✗) next to the things the reviewer did not write about.**

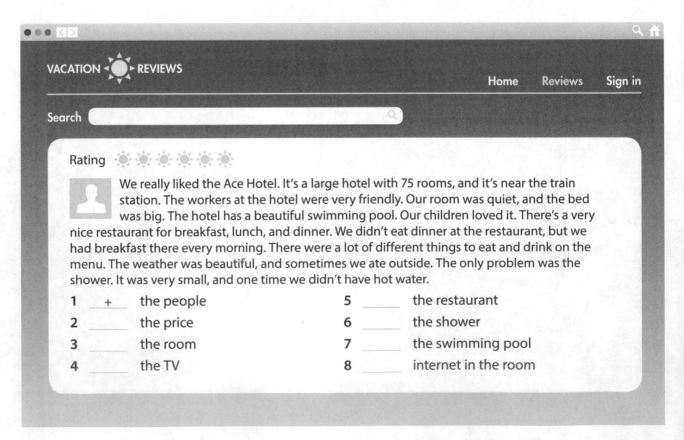

VACATION REVIEWS   Home   Reviews   Sign in

Search

Rating ☀ ☀ ☀ ☀ ☀ ☀

We really liked the Ace Hotel. It's a large hotel with 75 rooms, and it's near the train station. The workers at the hotel were very friendly. Our room was quiet, and the bed was big. The hotel has a beautiful swimming pool. Our children loved it. There's a very nice restaurant for breakfast, lunch, and dinner. We didn't eat dinner at the restaurant, but we had breakfast there every morning. There were a lot of different things to eat and drink on the menu. The weather was beautiful, and sometimes we ate outside. The only problem was the shower. It was very small, and one time we didn't have hot water.

1	_+_ the people	**5**	_____	the restaurant
2	_____ the price	**6**	_____	the shower
3	_____ the room	**7**	_____	the swimming pool
4	_____ the TV	**8**	_____	internet in the room

WRITING

A **Add commas to the sentences when necessary.**

1 We stayed at the hotel on Monday, Tuesday, and Wednesday.

2 The room was noisy and small.

3 We had lunch and dinner at the hotel.

4 The hotel is near popular restaurants cafés and stores.

5 The busy months at my job are May June and July.

6 I went with my brother my sister and my cousin.

B **Read the questions and answers. Check (✓) when the speaker answers his or her own question.**

1 Where did you stay?   At a hotel near the beach.

2 Am I happy?   Of course, I'm happy.

3 Did I like the chocolate cake?   I loved the chocolate cake!

4 Do you want some pizza?   No, thank you. I'd like a sandwich.

C **Imagine you stayed at a hotel in your town. Write a review of the hotel. Describe the hotel and where it is. Say what is good (or bad) about the hotel.**

CHECK AND REVIEW

Read the statements. Can you do these things?

UNIT 12	Mark the boxes. ☑ I can do it. ? I am not sure. I can …	If you are not sure, go back to these pages in the Student's Book.
VOCABULARY	☐ use words for snacks and small meals. ☐ use words for food, drinks, and desserts.	page 118 page 120
GRAMMAR	☐ use the simple past in statements. ☐ use the simple past in *yes/no* and information questions. ☐ use *any*.	page 119 page 121 page 121
FUNCTIONAL LANGUAGE	☐ offer and request food and drink. ☐ use *so* and *really* to make words stronger.	page 122 page 123
SKILLS	☐ use commas in lists. ☐ write a hotel review.	page 125 page 125

EXTRA ACTIVITIES

7 TIME TO SPEAK Your life these days

A **Look online for books, movies, and songs.**

- What books are people reading these days?
- What movies are people watching these days?
- What songs are people listening to these days?

B **Write sentences and read to your class.**

8 TIME TO SPEAK National skills

A **People in these countries speak English. Choose <u>five</u> countries.**

- Australia
- Canada
- Ireland
- Jamaica
- New Zealand
- South Africa
- the United Kingdom
- the United States

B **Write sentences about what people in each country can do really well.**

C **Read your sentences to your class. Do other students agree?**

9 TIME TO SPEAK Vacation plans

A **Make travel plans.**

- Where do you want to go?
- What do you want to do?
- What do you need to do to travel there?

I want to go to San Diego … I want to swim and go to the zoo. I need to fly from my city.

B **Tell the class about your vacation plans.**

C **Do other students have different ideas?**

10 TIME TO SPEAK 48 hours in your city

A **Imagine a group of college students is going to visit your city next month. Plan 48 hours in your city for the group. Make a list of interesting things they can do in your city.**

B **Read your list to the class. Do you have the same ideas?**

11 TIME TO SPEAK TV memories

A **Talk to your family and friends about their favorite childhood TV shows.**

B **Go online and find information (names, places, things) about the shows.**

C **Write sentences about the shows.**

D **Read your sentences to your class. Did other students write sentences about the same shows?**

12 TIME TO SPEAK Recipe for a great restaurant

A **Look online for a restaurant you want to visit.**

B **Read reviews for the restaurant. What do people like about the restaurant? What do people <u>not</u> like?**

C **Show the restaurant website to the class. Tell the class about the reviewers' comments.**

The authors and publishers acknowledge the following sources of copyright material and are grateful for the permissions granted. While every effort has been made, it has not always been possible to identify the sources of all the material used, or to trace all copyright holders. If any omissions are brought to our notice, we will be happy to include the appropriate acknowledgements on reprinting and in the next update to the digital edition, as applicable.

Key: BL = Below Left, BR = Below Right, CL = Centre Left, T = Top, TR = Top Right.

Photo
All photos are sourced from Getty Images.

p. 50, p. 58 (photo 4), p. 58 (photo 12), p. 74: Westend61; p. 51, p. 85 (girl): Hero Images; p. 52: M_a_y_a/E+; p. 54: DMEPhotography/iStock/ Getty Images Plus; p. 55: Fresh Meat Media LLC/The Image Bank; p. 56: Jim Craigmyle/Corbis; p. 58 (photo 1): Efenzi/E+; p. 58 (photo 2): Ruth Jenkinson/Dorling Kindersley; p. 58 (photo 3): Flyfloor/E+; p. 58 (photo 5): MCCAIG/iStock/Getty Images Plus; p. 58 (photo 6): otnaydur/Shutterstock; p. 58 (photo 7): Kevin Smith/Perspectives; p. 58 (photo 8): Jerry Driendl/The Image Bank; p. 58 (photo 9): JGI/Blend Images; p. 58 (photo 10): Caiaimage/Sam Edwards/OJO+; p. 58 (photo 11): Jose Luis Pelaez Inc/Blend Images; p.58 (waves): Specker/Vedfelt/Taxi; p. 60: Skynesher/E+; p. 61: Monkeybusinessimages/iStock/Getty Images Plus; p. 62: PeopleImages/E+; p. 63: Steve Debenport/iStock/Getty Images Plus; p. 64: Kohei Hara/DigitalVision; p. 66: Tim Boyle/Getty Images; p. 67 (TR): Saro17/E+; p. 67 (CL): RachelDewis/iStock/Getty Images Plus; p. 67 (BR): Jose Fuste Raga/Corbis Documentary; p. 68: Studio 504/Stone; p. 69: Marco Brivio/Photographer's Choice RF; p. 70: Hiya Images/Corbis/ VCG/Corbis; p. 71, p. 92: Andresr/E+; p. 72: GUY Christian/Hemis.fr; p. 75: Troy Aossey/Taxi; p. 76: Seanscott/RooM; p. 77: 97/E+; p. 78: Seb Oliver/Image Source; p. 80 (T): Bjorn Andren; p. 80 (BL): NightAndDayImages/E+; p. 80 (BR): Ken Ross/VW Pics/UIG/Getty Images; p. 82: Erik Isakson/Blend Images; p. 83: JTB Photo/UIG/Getty Images; p. 84: Daniele Carotenuto Photography/Moment; p. 85 (shoe): Peter Dazeley/ Photographer's Choice; p. 86: Thomas Barwick/Taxi; p. 87: Luis Alvarez/ Taxi; p. 88: Switch/ailead/amana images; p. 90: GUIZIOU Franck/ hemispicture.com/hemis.fr; p. 91: David Nevala/Aurora; p. 93 (T): Eileen Bach/Iconica; p. 93 (BR): Rosemary Calvert/Photographer's Choice RF; p. 94: Wavebreakmedia/iStock/Getty Images Plus; p. 95: Zoranm/E+; p. 96: LOOK Photography/UpperCut Images.

The following image is from other image library:

p. 58 (photo 6): otnaydur/Shutterstock.

Front cover photography by Arctic-Images/The Image Bank/Getty Images.

Audio production by CityVox, New York.

Corpus
Development of this publication has made use of the Cambridge English Corpus (CEC). The CEC is a multi-billion word collection of contemporary spoken and written English. It includes British English, American English, and other varieties. It also includes the Cambridge Learner Corpus, the world's biggest collection of learner writing, developed in collaboration with Cambridge Assessment. Cambridge University Press uses the CEC to provide evidence about language use that helps to produce better language teaching materials.

Our Evolve authors study the Corpus to see how English is really used, and to identify typical learner mistakes. This information informs the authors' selection of vocabulary, grammar items and Student's Book Corpus features such as the Accuracy Check, Register Check, and Insider English.